For Betty and Graham Hines

S o cold it was:

by late December, ink had frosted
in its well; my breath was tinkling
on my lips, so everything I saw to tell
I had to memorise. I saw birds
fall from trees, too stiff to fly, like stones.
I saw a lass, her tongue stuck to a spoon.
I saw an ice-hare staring lifeless at no moon.

All this as I walked from Spitalfields
by way of London Bridge to Southwark, dressed
as a man for reasons of my own; a poet-spy;

by late December, ink had frosted
in its well; my breath was tinkling
on my lips, so everything I saw to tell
I had to memorise. I saw birds
fall from trees, too stiff to fly, like stones.
I saw a lass, her tongue stuck to a spoon.
I saw an ice-hare staring lifeless at no moon.

So cold it was:

Anon. At Bishopsgate, I fell in with a crowd
all streaming south. I saw a frozen cat
arched on a wall; a lad kicking a silvered rat;
and not one chilly citizen could doff his hat.

London was snow. St Paul's, a talent of the snow
to seem more grand. The bells hung in their towers,
dumb. Trees went to pieces; cracked. Men's tears
were jewels in their beards for wives to pluck.
I saw a spider's web enriched with rime.
I saw a clock too cold to tell the time;
a pickpocket's hand too blue to do the crime.

The air more cruel, it nipped and bit me
to a tavern, where I ordered up mulled wine
and listened in. A sailor spoke of how the sea
lay fettered to the shore. A sad-faced jester
warmed his chittering monkey at the fire.
I saw a barefoot vagrant enter, pale
as death, and beg for bread, and fail.
I saw the monkey sink a pint of ale.

At Billingsgate, fishwives threw fistfights
and the fishermen were drunk as eels;
the empty nets heaped in their frigid chains.

One wailed his boat was crushed to sticks.
One swore he'd spied a dolphin, turned to lead
upon a moveless wave; so help him God.
I saw him charge a crown for a cod.

I mused on climate — how it could clench
the greatest city in its bitter fist
and squeeze. For now I stood on London Bridge,
next to a man with walrus for a face,
beside a bawd whose eyes were hard as gems.
My mouth as wide as one at Bethlehem's,
I saw another town on the Thames.

Where men had drowned, there stretched
whole streets of booths. A coach and six drove down
the central avenue. Folk slid and skated
on the ice. Large boats were drawn by mules.

Tents waved with flags. I saw a bear
surrounded by a boozy mob; by Temple Stairs,
jugglers on stilts proclaimed a travelling fair.

I walked on water; heard my steps click
on its thickened back; slipped on my arse.
Vendors sold gingerbread, black pudding, snuff,
plum cake, brandy balls, hot pudding, pies.
I found a Fuddling Tent and drank spiced rum.
I saw a wheeled boat with a youth banging a drum.
I saw a fox-hunt; fire-eater; football scrum.

I met a wench who thought I was a man,
or didn't care, and stole a salty kiss.
I've never seen her since. I tossed a coin
to watch a man swallow his sword. I paid a sixpence
to a printer for my name, the place, the date, the year,
to truly certify that I was here.
I saw a piglet roasted on a spear.

And everywhere, a vital human thrum
as if no one would ever die; the wild faces
of a carnival, all in their cups; mad freedom
from the usual. I saw a couple married
by a tipsy priest, exchanging rings of ice
carved by a silversmith. I bought a necklace
on a whim, which didn't melt till Candlemas.

The frail shy sun, a cloistered nun, faded
and vanished. The river was the moon's
to flatter more; embellish upheaved floes
to crystal walls; sparkle St Paul's.

I saw a hundred dancing fires lit.
I saw a whole ox turning on a spit
and swapped a shilling for a steaming slice of it.

I skidded to a fortune-teller's booth
and had my palm read there by candlelight.
The one-eyed dame squinted my love and luck.
To celebrate, I took up with a group of players,
who sang and passed round brandy in a ring:
And folk do tipple without fear to sink
More liquor than the fish beneath do drink.

We stole the blankets which made up a shop;
laid out rough beds. And so it was, I slept
a whole night on the Thames, between
a farting Friar and a snoring Juliet.
I'm aching yet. I limp. I woke at dawn.
I saw the King upon the bridge, staring down;
a cap of glittering stalagmites for a crown.

Time to move on. The King had disappeared
when I climbed the bridge and made my eyes
commit a wonder to my heart. Two swans
alighted, swerving on the blazing glaze,
then flew, creaking, away. I spoke a prayer.
I saw my words freeze on the air
and hang, preserved, to thaw now in your ear.

Also by Carol Ann Duffy and available from Picador

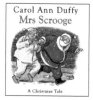

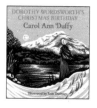